The Glory of Scotland

NUMBER ONE · THE WEST

JACK HOUSE

OLIVER AND BOYD

OLIVER AND BOYD
Tweeddale Court
Edinburgh 1
39A Welbeck Street
London, W.1
First published 1962

Colour Photographs by W. S. Thomson
Decorations by Pamela Mitchell and Robert Crawford
Designed and printed by Robert MacLehose and Company Limited
Glasgow W.3. Scotland

Introduction

No country is perfect, not even—if I dare say so—the U.S.A. or the U.S.S.R. But I suggest that Scotland, from the eye-view (or *your* point of view) is just about as perfect as you'll ever see. This is not an idle suggestion. It is backed up with pictures which tell, as no words could do, of the glory of the West of Scotland. Believe me, the other parts of Scotland are beautiful and majestic and intriguing too.

For me, of course, the best part of this incomparable country is the land in the West. I should say the land and the water in the West, for the geographical aspect which makes the West different from the rest of Scotland is that there is at least as much water as land in its make-up. The only other country I know which has so much water is Finland, but, beautiful though it is, it does not have the mountains and the fiords and the terrible cliffs which line the West coast of Scotland.

I said 'for me, of course', and I had better explain that. I am a Glaswegian, a citizen of the finest town in the world. So I am thirled to the West, even though I also admire the beautiful bleakness of the North, the lively ambience of the East, and the rolling cosiness of the Borders and Galloway in the South.

There is no better starting-off place for seeing the Glory of the West than the city of Glasgow. Cynics say that the great thing about Glasgow is that it's so easy to get out of! Unlike so many cynicisms, that is true. Within an hour from Glasgow you can be in the Highlands, or you can be in that world-famous estuary, the Firth of Clyde, or you can be in the Burns Country. Within an hour you can even be in Edinburgh!

Despite what I have just said—and you may well think it strange!—there is no picture of Glasgow in this Glory of the West. That is not because Glasgow hasn't beauty. It might well come into this collection because, as you will see, this is a record of the flowers of Scotland. Most of our visitors know Scotland as a land of romance and adventure, of song and story, and it has also a reputation as 'The Land o' Cakes'. But few realise that, though Scotland is famous for its mountains and glens and lochs and wildness, it is full of flowers.

Glasgow is full of flowers too. The city has more public parks per head of population than any other in the entire world. In one park alone, Queen's Park, there are more flowers than in the five Royal Parks of Paris put together.

I mention this especially because Glasgow's reputation outside Glasgow seems to rest on razor-slashers in the Gorbals, tough men building gigantic liners on Clydeside, the 'worst slums in Europe' (though there are just as bad in Copenhagen), and interminable rain descending on soot-covered buildings.

There is one good thing about this kind of reputation. When people *do* visit Glasgow they are not only pleasantly surprised, they are so astonished that they often make Glaswegians blush with their praises.

In the compass of this book, then, it is inevitable that we have shown only part of the Glory of the West. It would take many books such as this to tell the whole story in pictures of this wonderful country. We start in the South in Ayrshire and move up the Western coast of Scotland to the North-West tip of Great Britain, Cape Wrath. But, while we show you scenes in Ayrshire, on the Firth of Clyde, on the Isle of Arran, and the bonnie banks of Loch Lomond, we haven't the space for the handsome Mull of Kintyre, or such delightful islands as Gigha, Islay and Jura.

As we go North, we run into the same trouble. Coll and Tiree are not represented here, nor that string of islands which come nearest to the American saying, 'out of this world'—Barra, Eriskay, South Uist, Benbecula and North Uist.

The simple fact is that the West of Scotland is so glorious that the best a poor book publisher can do is to make a selection from the wonderful pictures which are available, and hope that it will inspire the visitor with the camera and the colour film to see even more than is shown in this volume.

That is why my text, running alongside the pictures, tells you more than just the subject of the photograph itself. This, I hope, is a practical as well as a beautiful book. There are maps to show you the other glories in the West.

You can see the Glory of the West by land, air and sea, and each has its own peculiar advantages. My Clyde sailing friends tell me that it's quite impossible to appreciate the islands, the long sea lochs and the mainland mountains without seeing them from the sea. They really mean sailing in a yacht. For myself, the island steamers are good enough. But I must also say a word for seeing the West from the air.

I'll never forget a trip I once did from Renfrew (the airport for Glasgow) to Stornoway. It was a wonderful day in early Spring and, once we'd got clear of Argyll's Bowling Green, the mountains behind the Holy Loch, we had nothing high in our way. So our pilot skimmed over the islands. In fact, we were flying at about 500 feet, but it seemed much lower.

I have flown over the North Pole, across the Alps, parallel with the Rockies, and through the Caucasus mountains in Russia. Apart from the North Pole, which is deadly dull, these were flights of great beauty. But I have yet to fly amid such surpassing loveliness as on that day over the Western Isles.

Most people, I imagine, will travel through the glorious West by land. You can cover nearly all this ground, even including the islands if you are determined and the tide is right for loading and unloading, by car. There are also trains from Glasgow which link with steamers, and the train run (again from Glasgow) by Fort William to Mallaig is one of such beauty that British Railways run special excursions for photographers!

As far as the South-West is concerned, travel is easy. There are trains to all the principal places and the Firth of Clyde is laced with steamers and car ferries. The car ferry is comparatively modern and it is revolutionising travel around the Clyde. Where British Railways, in the form of the Caledonian Steam Packet Company, expected to carry hundreds, they are transporting thousands of cars.

The roads are good but very busy in the holiday seasons. Since there is only one road (the Western one) which follows the bonnie, bonnie banks o' Loch Lomond, it tends to become something of a bottle-neck. But, once you get North of Loch Lomond, traffic eases. Even owners of huge American cars need not worry until they go North of Fort William. Then many roads are single-track affairs, with passing places marked by a diamond lozenge on a post every 100 yards or so.

If you really choose to go into the wilds, don't take a long car. You are just asking for trouble if you do. Quite apart from the narrow and tortuous roads, there are wee bridges over burns and every now and then a low-slung, long car grounds, as it were, on the hump back of such a bridge.

There are few straight roads up in the West. The sea lochs poke their fingers into the mainland and you may have to take a very roundabout route to some place which the crow could fly to in a nice straight line in a fraction of your time. Here and there you'll find car ferries. In some cases it's essential to cross by the car ferry, though in the height of the season this may involve a long, long wait. In cases where there is an alternative road (such as at Ballachulish on Loch Leven), the run round the loch is so beautiful that you feel the extra time taken is well worth it.

The Scots are one of the nations which persistently run down their own weather, so, if you are a visitor, you may well have some rather strange ideas of what to expect. Even our neighbours, the English, imagine that we live in a miasma of rain in the summer and a perpetual blizzard in the winter. It's not so long ago that a London film company sent up a unit to a place on the Firth of Clyde to do some background shooting. The amount of film wanted was about one and a half minute's worth, and the assistant director in charge of the unit was told that he would have three weeks to shoot this. But, if the weather was what the director of the film expected, the assistant director could have three more weeks.

The unit came to the Clyde, fully equipped for severe winter conditions although the month was May. To their intense surprise the weather was so perfect that they had completed all their shooting and were back in London in three days.

I am not suggesting that the weather will be perfect for you. Indeed, I will go so far as to suggest that anybody coming to the West of Scotland for the first time should prepare for rain, in a reasonable sort of way. And, since a good deal of your travelling around the West may well be by sea, you would be wise to bring some warm clothes with you too. No matter how warm the day may be, a steamer deck can be draughty at times.

When I write these words to our visitors, I am really looking over my shoulders at the Scots who have bought this book. The Scots are, on the whole, convinced that we have worse weather than anywhere else and, even if you trot out the statistics to show that during those three weeks of solid rain on the Riviera, the sun shone every day on the Island of Tiree, they refuse to be impressed.

The visitors I have met in the West of Scotland take quite a different view. I was with two Sassenachs (Gaelic for Englishmen, Southerners or visitors) on their first day on the Isle of Skye. The rain was pouring down and the Coolins were hidden in mist. I said I was sorry that this should be their first view of Skye. 'Sorry?' said the husband. 'But this is just what we wanted to see. Look at those streams coming hurtling down the hillside. Look at that waterfall. This is magnificent!'

After that, I hadn't the heart to tell him that the streams were really burns. Next day, incidentally, was a gloriously sunny one and the happy Sassenachs saw the island under ideal conditions.

The Scots, of course, are the greatest critics of the Scots and Scotland ever known. Where other nationals stand up for their country, and even praise it extravagantly, the Scots are telling the world about Scotland's awful weather and bad roads and dreadful hotels and dismal service. Well, you can find all these things in Scotland, just as you can find them anywhere else. But up and down the West of Scotland I have eaten and lived in some of the best hotels I have encountered anywhere.

If you are following the route of this book, you will be spending most of your time in the Highlands. The general idea, even among many Scots, is that Scotland is divided by a horizontal line, running somewhere across Stirling, with the Lowlands to the South of it and the Highlands to the North.

But the real division is diagonal, and the line of demarcation runs from the Firth of Clyde right up to Aberdeen. The East side of the Firth of Clyde is Lowland. The West side is Highland. Even yet there is still a Gaelic speaker or two in the Isle of Arran and on the Cowal coast.

Despite easier travelling, inter-marrying and 'blanket'-style education, the Highlanders are still a race apart. Although their language, the Gaelic, is supposed to be declining every year, you will still hear it used all over the Highlands, and particularly in the Islands. The other day I stood at a bar counter in Lochmaddy Hotel on North Uist. A partition divides the public bar from the lounge bar, but it's all the same counter. The barmaid, I noticed, spoke English on the lounge bar side and Gaelic on the public bar side!

Gaelic is a very ancient tongue, so ancient indeed that some people say that it was the language which Adam and Eve used in the Garden of Eden. If you are lucky, you may be invited to a *ceilidh*, which is a gathering where Gaelic songs are sung and old stories retold.

You will find the Highlanders courteous, soft-spoken and maybe a shade reserved. They have long memories in the Highlands and perhaps they'll still be thinking of some Clan feud, or the dreadful things which were done after the Jacobite cause was defeated at the Battle of Culloden, or the Clearances, when whole townships were transported to Canada. Or possibly they're just thinking of the price their sheep will get at the next market.

The farther North you go into the West, the fewer hotels there are, and it's unwise to depend on chance for getting accommodation for the night. But recently there has been an enormous increase in the number of places offering 'Bed and Breakfast'. Many Highland crofts now give that service, and I have yet to meet a visitor who has been disappointed. Most crofters combine farming with fishing, so that their guests may be offered the kind of fresh food from the land or the loch which is hard to find in these deep-freeze days.

North of Oban you find the Highland temperament changing. There is a good deal of letting tomorrow take care of itself, particularly out in the Western Isles. There is probably no other part of Scotland where it is so easy to relax as in those islands. It would seem that the pushing type of Highlander makes for the South. (Glasgow, they say, has the biggest Highland population of any place in the world.) The Highlanders who are left behind take things calmly. It's wonderful to hear an elderly Highlander say, 'Yes, man, when the Good Lord made time, he made plenty of it!'

There are sometimes exceptions to this Highland calmness. You must be careful not to offend religious susceptibilities in the Highlands. Once, staying at a hotel on one of the little islands south of Mull, I went out on a Sunday morning and tapped about a golf ball with a golf club on the front lawn. I wasn't exactly run out of town, but the disapproval made itself strongly felt.

Later in this book I mention the 'Long Island', that chain of Western isles which starts with Barra and goes right up to Lewis. In the 'Long Island' the changes in religious faith from one place to another are quite remarkable. I'm told that Barra is 100 per cent Roman Catholic. Just across the water is South Uist, which is 95 per cent Catholic and 5 per cent Protestant. Then comes Benbecula, which is 50–50. Across the causeway there is North Uist, and the proportion becomes 95 per cent Protestant and 5 per cent Catholic. There are similar differences between Harris and Lewis, and right up by Stornoway and the North of Lewis the much reported 'Wee Frees' exert great authority.

Detailing these differences makes me realise that I may have been guilty in these pages of generalising rather too much about the Highlanders. There are all kinds of Highlanders, just as there are all kinds of Lowlanders and Englishmen and Welshmen.

Perhaps I could illustrate this point with a favourite Highland story. The people of South Uist find it difficult to pronounce 'th'. They describe their island as 'Souse Uist'. The numbers 13 and 30 are 'sirteen' and 'sirty' to them.

The story goes that a South Uist skipper was taking his boat into the harbour at Lochboisdale when there was a cry from the water—'Help, help! I'm sinking, I'm sinking!' The skipper paid no attention, and the voice in the darkness shouted, 'Do you hear me? I'm sinking, I'm sinking!'

'Yes, yes, I hear you,' replied the skipper over the side of the boat. 'But what is it that you are sinking about?'

Well, I am sinking—I mean, thinking—that I have told you as much as you need to know to enjoy yourself in the glorious West of Scotland. This part of the world is unique. For colour it is unsurpassed, even if it does happen to be raining. People who have visited the Western Highlands and the Western Isles once come back year after year.

And they are welcomed year after year. There is nothing quite so heartfelt as a Highland welcome. The host and guest tradition is still as strong in the Highlands as ever it was.

Am I being too ecstatic? I trust not. Of course there are exceptions. All hosts and all guests don't get on well together. Everything in the garden isn't always rosy, even in the beautiful gardens of the West.

I will end on a corrective note. Two English ladies were admiring a fine collie belonging to a Highland shepherd. In that delightfully extravagant English way they were praising it to the sky—it was a wonderful dog, a magnificent beast, look at the intelligence in its eyes, and so on and so on. The old shepherd stood it as long as he could, and then he said, 'Well, well, now. He's a dog all right. He's a good dog. But he's no' a *helluva* dog!'

Whether you've bought this book to see what you're going to see, or to be reminded of what you've seen, or to send to somebody else to show them what they ought to see —enjoy yourself!

The Glory of the West

1. Brig o' Doon, Ayr

We'd better get things clear, right at the start. The old Brig o' Doon at Alloway, near Ayr, is not—repeat, *not*—the site of a village named Brigadoon which appears only once every 100 years! Many American, Canadian, and even English visitors to Scotland go to see the Brig o' Doon because they have already seen the musical play, made into a musical film, *Brigadoon*. But Brigadoon exists only in the imagination of the American writers of the script.

The real Brig o' Doon is the ancient stone bridge over the River Doon, and it owes its fame to one of the world's great poets, Robert Burns. Many people consider his best poem is *Tam o' Shanter*, which describes the midnight ride of the happy farmer from the inn at Ayr to the auld kirk at Alloway, where he surprised the Devil himself playing the bagpipes for a dance of witches.

Most of the witches were the traditional withered hags, but there was one young woman among them, and she took Tam's eye. She was wearing a short chemise which showed her figure at its best. In Scots a short chemise is a 'cutty sark', and Tam o' Shanter, carried away by the sight, shouted, 'Weel done, Cutty Sark!' And in an instant all was dark.

Then out flew the hellish legion after Tam, who knew that he could escape in only one way—across running water. Witches cannot cross running water, and the nearest was the River Doon. So his grey mare Meg, knowing well that her master was in dire danger, galloped her best to the Brig o' Doon. The witches, led by Cutty Sark, were closing upon the horse and rider. But Meg was a mettlesome steed. Just as Cutty Sark caught her by the tail, Meg gave a great leap and crossed the keystone of the bridge.

The tail came off in Cutty Sark's hands, but Tam o' Shanter was safe.

You can walk down the cobbles between the Burns Monument Hotel and the Burns Monument, an imitation Grecian temple, and climb the tall, slender arch until you stand at the very spot where Meg made her vital bound and lost her tail. And you can look up and down the river, and remember one of Robert Burns' most famous songs—

> Ye banks and braes o' bonnie Doon,
> How can ye bloom sae fresh and fair?

This is the centre of the Burns Country. You can rest in the Banks o' Doon tea gardens, with a view of the old brig and the Doon running softly over the stones below you. Or you can visit the Burns Monument and see such mementoes of the poet as his wife's wedding ring, and the Bible which he was said to have used when he married Highland Mary by holding hands across running water and swearing to be true. Running water is a valuable commodity in Scotland. It's used for marrying, stopping witches, and making whisky.

Not far from the Brig o' Doon is Kirk Alloway, still a sinister ruin, and the 'auld clay biggin' in which Robert Burns was born on January 25th, 1759. Some 100,000 people visit Burns' Cottage every year. Among them have been Queen Elizabeth, Malenkov, Joe Louis, Dr Wellington Koo, President Eisenhower, the Duke of Windsor, Clark Gable, the Duke of Edinburgh, and Irving Berlin.

The thatched cottage is still much the same as when Robert's father built it, but the original road ran on the other side of the clay biggin and from the present day road you are looking at the back of the house. It's a simple but and ben, with a few Burns relics in it. Across the garden is the Burns Museum with a priceless collection of Burnsiana.

2. Brodick, Arran

Brodick has the principal pier of the Isle of Arran, the largest island in the Firth of Clyde. The voyage by steamer or car ferry (that's a car ferry in our picture) takes less than an hour from Ardrossan or Fairlie. Indeed, the whole journey by train and boat from Glasgow is accomplished in about two hours. Yet, outside the summer holiday season, Arran seems almost as remote as the far-off Western Isles.

Across Brodick Bay is Brodick Castle, once the home of the last owner of the island, the late Duchess of Montrose, and now under the administration of the National Trust for Scotland. Its treasures are now open to the public, and in the spring and early summer the gardens, with their wonderful display of sub-tropical plants and rhododendrons, are well worth a visit.

Above Brodick Castle broods Arran's highest mountain, Goatfell (2,866 feet). When there's snow on the mountain top, Goatfell is uncannily like Mount Fujiyama. Incidentally, Goatfell's name has nothing to do with goats, although you may see some near the top. It is derived from the Gaelic and means 'Mountain of the winds'.

Behind Goatfell are the Arran Alps, which offer some of the finest climbing in Scotland. Because they are not as high as some other mountains, the Arran peaks are sometimes attempted by ill-equipped climbers. Not only do these neophytes suffer in consequence, but they cause a great deal of trouble to the Brodick and Corrie men who have to go up to rescue them.

The road round Arran is less than 60 miles long, but a car run will show you a sort of Wagnerian back-drop of mountains in the north, running down to golden beaches and palm trees in the south. Arran has often been called 'the epitome of Scotland', because every kind of scenery on the mainland is to be seen on this island. It is also a sort of geological freak, because almost every geological formation in the British Isles is found here.

The population of Arran is about 5,000, and it's said that there are at least as many deer as people on the island. If you go round the north, by Corrie and Sannox to Lochranza, where Prime Minister Macmillan's ancestors lived, you may see the white stag. Arran is a very superstitious place and the old people say that a white stag is always seen before the death of the laird. This white stag was first sighted shortly before the death of the Duchess of Montrose.

Arran is an island with its own fairies. There are not only the well-known brownies, but also bocans and bleaters. The bocans are rough, tough gnomes. The bleaters are a kind of zombie. A bleater will come into your house, sit by the fire, and weep all night.

For more than 100 years Arran has been a great holiday centre for Glasgow and West of Scotland people, although it is anything but a holiday resort in the popular sense of the term. It consists of villages and clachans, spaced out along its sixty miles of road, and each of them has its own admirers, who go there faithfully year after year and consider that the place of their choice is the only one worth visiting.

At one time it was known as Jack Buchanan's island, because that star of musical comedy spent a holiday there every year. Tomorrow it may well be known as Dorothy Tutin's island, because that brilliant young actress visits Arran every time she gets the chance.

Yachting on the Clyde

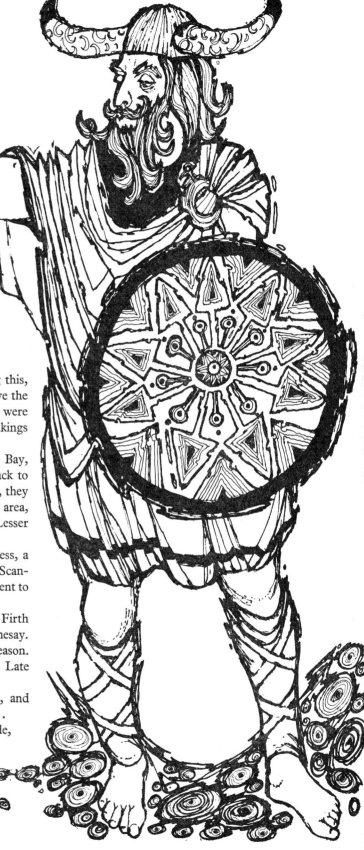

The Firth of Clyde, regarded by most Scots as the finest estuary in the world, is really a miniature sea. On one side is the Scottish mainland; on the other, the long fingers of the coasts of Kintyre and Argyll. And in between are 1,240 square miles of salt water. This gives plenty of space for giant liners (the *Queen Mary* and the *Queen Elizabeth* were launched on the Clyde and did their trials on the Firth), immense oil tankers, cargo ships, pleasure steamers, wee puffers and yachts of all shapes and sizes.

The Clyde Fortnight is one of the big events of the international yachtsman's world, and the yachtsmen come here from America, Scandinavia, France, Ireland and Germany to compete. The whole Firth is ringed by yacht clubs and, until lately, Hunter's Quay, where this picture was taken, was the headquarters of the Royal Clyde Yacht Club, which has 650 members.

There is a yachting school at Blairmore, not far from the Holy Loch, where the American Navy have their Polaris base. And in this area, and up by the Gareloch, there are some of the finest yacht builders in Britain.

Although the Firth of Clyde is an inland sea, it can be just as rough as the Atlantic, on the other side of the Mull of Kintyre. There are times when the car ferries and passenger steamers cannot sail. A number of ships have been wrecked in the Clyde because their skippers underestimated the strength of this stretch of water. And it's due to the Clyde weather that Scotland is part of Britain today and not under the ownership of Norway.

In 1263 King Haakon of Norway, who had already captured the Western Isles and was laying claim to the mainland of Scotland, brought a gigantic Viking fleet round Cape Wrath and down the very track this book is describing, into the Firth of Clyde. The Viking galleys lay in the Firth all the way from the Holy Loch in the north to Arran in the south.

King Alexander III of Scotland mustered his army at Largs and prepared to repel invaders. It was not thought by the military experts that he had much of a chance. But a tremendous storm blew up and the Firth of Clyde was turned into a series of churning whirlpools. Some of Haakon's ships were driven ashore and the Vikings who landed were immediately attacked by Alexander's soldiers. Seeing this, Haakon decided to make the best of a bad job and gave the order for a general attack. But in the storm his orders were lost, many ships were destroyed, and eventually the Vikings had to retreat.

Haakon remustered his broken fleet in Lamlash Bay, between the Holy Isle and Arran. Then he sailed back to Norway and died soon afterwards—of a broken heart, they say. Many of his Viking warriors were buried in this area, particularly on the two islands, the Greater and the Lesser Cumbrae.

At Largs there's a monument to Alexander's success, a slim tower built where the battle was fiercest. But Scandinavians are welcome at Largs today, and the monument to the battle is known locally as 'The Pencil'.

Largs is one of the many holiday places around the Firth of Clyde. It shares the lead with Dunoon and Rothesay. Each of these towns trebles its population in the season. Although they are so popular, the towns are still Late Victorian in appearance.

Harry Lauder lived for a long time at Dunoon, and sometimes I fancy I can still hear him there, singing . . .

Roamin' in the gloamin', on the bonny banks o' Clyde,
Roamin' in the gloamin', wi' a lassie by my side.

4. Loch Lomond

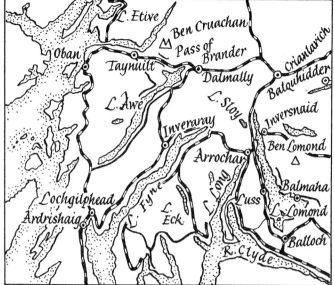

Loch Lomond is not only the biggest loch in Scotland, but the largest sheet of inland water in Britain. It is twenty-four miles long and five miles broad at the Balloch, or southern end, narrowing to about three-quarters of a mile half-way up. In the thirties the late Kaye Don set up a world water speed record on Loch Lomond.

A favourite riddle in Scotland is, 'What piece of water surrounds a foot?' The answer is Loch Lomond, because it has twelve inches in it. Inch is the Scottish word for an island, and among the islands you can see from the bonnie banks are Inchmurrin, Inchcailloch, Inchtavannach and Inchfad. In the interests of accuracy, it must be stated that there are some thirty islands in the loch, and at least thirteen of them bear the prefix or suffix, Inch.

A good road, though rather narrow for the traffic it has to take, runs up the western side of Loch Lomond. On the eastern side the road runs only to Rowardennan, where you can start the climb to the top of Ben Lomond (3,192 feet).

The best way to see the bonnie banks is from the loch itself. A 555-ton paddle steamer, *Maid of the Loch*, runs regularly throughout the summer from Balloch Pier. Motor boats ply from Balloch and Balmaha, but they don't go beyond the archipelago of Inches at the south of the loch. The *Maid* sails right up to Ardlui at the top of the loch, and touches at various piers on the way. It's possible to take the steamer to Rowardennan, climb Ben Lomond, and be back down in time to board it again for Balloch.

Loch Lomond, world famed nowadays for its beauty, was more noted for battles in the Good Old Days. The Vikings sailed up Loch Long to where Arrochar stands today, pulled their war galleys across the hill a mile or so to Tarbet on Loch Lomond, relaunched the ships, and then spent happy days sailing up and down the loch sacking, burning and looting. After the Vikings were defeated at the Battle of Largs, the Scots came into their own, and the MacGregor, MacFarlane and Colquhoun clans fought each other all round Loch Lomond.

The MacGregors and MacFarlanes have gone, but Sir Ivar Colquhoun is the Laird of Luss today. The MacFarlanes were the clan who 'had the moon for a lantern', a reference to their night raiding habits. In 1603 the MacGregors massacred the Colquhouns in Glen Fruin, not far from Balloch, and were pronounced nameless and landless.

The most famous MacGregor, of course, was Rob Roy, who was either an outlaw, a patriot, a cattle thief or a hero, according to the way you look at it. At Inversnaid you can see Rob Roy's Cave (which Robert the Bruce also occupied), and between Inversnaid and Rowardennan there is another cave called Rob Roy's Prison.

Rob was a famous swordsman, perhaps because of his long arms. It was said that he could tie his garters without stooping. I have handled his whisky bottle and my two hands could hardly grasp what he held in one. Although he was such a warrior, he died peacefully in his bed at Balquhidder in 1734.

The *Maid of the Loch* sailors will point out to you the places linked with Rob Roy, but you'll also see the water-ski-ing off Arden and Inchmurrin, the great caravan camp near Balmaha, a fine selection of youth hostels, and the Loch Lomond end of the Loch Sloy hydro-electric scheme.

5. Loch Awe

'It's a far cry to Loch Awe!' the Campbells used to say when they wanted to anger their enemies. For any opponent who wanted to try conclusions with the Campbells had to seek them out at their ancient stronghold, Kilchurn Castle on Loch Awe, in the midst of some of the wildest country in the wild Highlands.

The taunt means nothing now. You can get to Loch Awe easily from the south, by Loch Craignish and the village of Ford, or from the north by Dalmally. And many people take the far cry to Loch Awe because it is so famous for its fishing and its scenery and, in recent times, for its pony trekking. A hydro-electric scheme is planned for the loch, but the authorities promise that it will not affect adversely the fishing, the scenery or the pony trekking.

Loch Awe is long and narrow, except at its northern end, where it is dotted with islands. Kilchurn Castle stands on a promontory at this end and it is said to date from 1440. One of the Campbells, Sir Colin, left it to go to the Crusades, where he became a Knight of Rhodes. He was away so long that his wife gave him up for dead. She rebuilt Kilchurn and planned to marry again. But Sir Colin returned, just in time for the wedding. His wife didn't recognise him but, when she handed this 'stranger' some wine, he dropped his ring into the glass.

Among the islands are Inishail, the 'isle of rest', on which are the ruins of the church of St Pindoca and a burial ground of the MacArthur Clan. Another isle is Fraoch Eilean ('heather island'), named after the great Celtic hero, Fraoch, who was a notable slayer of dragons. There are the remains of a royal castle on Fraoch Eilean.

Among the villages on either side of the loch is one called New York. As far as I can gather, this is the same sort of 'sport' as the village of Moscow, near Kilmarnock, or the California, near Falkirk. You should pay a special visit to St Conan's Kirk, one of the most beautiful little churches in Scotland.

The twin peaks of Ben Cruachan (3,689 feet) tower above the north end of Loch Awe. The climb is not difficult and you can start either from Dalmally or Taynuilt. From the summit you can see Ben Nevis to the north, the Coolins in Skye, the Outer Hebrides and the headlands of Mull—if it's a clear day!

An arm of Loch Awe narrows to the west and the Pass of Brander and, through this awesome gash, the River Awe flows into Loch Etive. Here Robert the Bruce defeated the MacDougalls of Lorn, who were his rivals for the crown of Scotland. South Lorn lies between Loch Craignish, Loch Awe and Loch Etive.

Taynuilt on Loch Etive is a charming village, but it was once a Scottish industrial centre. Iron ore was once smelted by charcoal, which came mainly from oak. About the end of the 18th century the Government forbade the use of oak in England for charcoal, because they wanted the wood for their ships of oak. Taynuilt was famous for its oaks and beeches, so many English iron-workers came north to Taynuilt. There are still English names in these parts.

Behind Taynuilt Parish Kirk is the first monument ever erected to Admiral Lord Nelson. When the English iron-workers heard of the victory at Trafalgar they set up an old standing stone and engraved it in Nelson's honour.

Across Loch Etive from Taynuilt is Bonawe where, every few years, the biggest blast in Britain is heard. This is at the granite quarry, and some of the most notable parts of London are paved with Bonawe granite.

The Clans

There are many Clan societies in Scotland today, and nearly every Clan has a recognised Chief. But the old Clan system is dead. It could not survive the stern repression of the British Government after the Battle of Culloden in 1746. The Clan chiefs who were 'out' with Bonnie Prince Charlie had their lands taken from them, and without land a Clan lost its purpose.

Could the Clans not have waited until their Chiefs returned? Some of them did. But many Highland people were forced out of Scotland, and many more had to go because there was nothing to live on. The 'wealth' of a Clan lay in its herds of black cattle (which, by the way, weren't necessarily black). After Culloden the Government troops seized the Clans' cattle wherever they found the beasts, and sent them south.

The Americans did much the same to the Red Indians. They found that hunting down and exterminating the buffalo, the Indians' 'wealth', brought the tribes into subjection much quicker than fighting them. Indeed, if you look into the organisation and life of the noble Red Man, you'll find a remarkable number of similarities with the old Scottish Clans.

Some people seem to imagine that Clan life was on the lines of the Squire and his tenantry in England. It was not in the least like that. A Clan was a family and, although the Chief had the power of life and death over his men, all were regarded as equal. If the Chief was the head of a big Clan, he had Chieftains below him, looking after other divisions of the family. The Chief wore a bonnet with three eagle's feathers in it; the Chieftain was allowed one eagle's feather.

Although the Highlanders were regarded as dreadful barbarians by the Lowlanders and the English, the Chiefs were all well educated men. Owing to the 'Auld Alliance' with France, they usually spoke French, along with Scots, English and the Gaelic. They vied with each other in 'showing off'. Any newspaper of, say, 1740 which tried to select 'The Ten Best-Dressed Men in the Highlands' would have had plenty of choice.

There is the famous story of the Highland Chief who, when he went to London, had a golden horseshoe specially made. When he took his first ride through the London streets, he had this shoe loosely fitted to one hoof of his horse. As they clattered along, the golden shoe came off, and the Londoners were awestruck by a Scotsman who, they thought, could afford to have his horse shod with gold.

A Clan Chief customarily had a personal bodyguard of the finest and strongest young men of the Clan. His entourage also included a standard bearer, a sword bearer, his personal servant, a harper, a bard, and a piper. If he was a very important Chief, there would also be a boy to carry the bagpipes for the piper.

The bard was a very essential member of this retinue. He knew the history of the Clan and kept adding to it with his own compositions. If feuding was to be done (and the Clan feuds were the fiercest ever known), the bard would recite the great deeds of the past and work up the Clansmen into a fury against their enemy.

Each Clan had its slogan and its badge and, once the Fiery Cross had been sent round, and the Clan had collected, the men would pin the badge (often a plant) to their bonnets and cry the Clan slogan fiercely. The Fiery Cross, by the way, is a misnomer. True, the cross was made and set alight, but then it was dipped in goat's blood, so that it merely smouldered on its way round the Clan country.

The Highlanders have always been known as terrible fighters. In the First World War the Germans, seeing them in the kilt, gave them the title of 'The Ladies from Hell'. After Culloden (and before it too), the Scots fought in all the armies of Europe and there are many Clan names even today in France, Russia and Scandinavia.

Yet in the old days Clan life had its gentle side too. The fighting men would number only about a fifth of the whole Clan and, if they were not fighting or cattle rieving, they'd be out hunting, or taking part in the kind of contest that we know today as the Highland Games. (This was to keep their strength up for the next fight!)

The rest of the Clan formed a complete community. Most of them would be employed in looking after the cattle or in growing oats and corn, fruit and vegetables. But there would also be joiners and blacksmiths and every other necessary kind of tradesman. Undoubtedly there would be at least one distiller.

This kind of life gradually died away after Culloden. Today there are many Clan societies in Scotland, and elsewhere in the world. But few of the present Clan Chiefs live on their Clan land, and the Clan societies spend most of their time perpetuating the former glories of their 'family' and holding meetings, dinners and gatherings. In some cases they give bursaries to help boys and girls of the Clan name.

And now, of course, you'll see outside those Tartan Shops which show a list of Clan and sept names ('If your name is here, you have a tartan!') people studying anxiously to see what tartan they can take. A recent list of Clan tartans numbered 109, although there were said to be not more than fifty Clans at the time of Culloden.

6. Inveraray Castle

In the old days the town of Inveraray nestled close to Inveraray Castle, and doubtless the first Earls and Dukes of Argyll liked their Campbell clansmen to be near them. You can't become the most powerful people in Scotland without making some enemies.

But the third Duke of Argyll felt that his castle was too small and too old, and that the inhabitants of Inveraray were too near him. So he engaged an architect to build him a new Inveraray Castle and a new Inveraray town, well away from the ducal seat. This piece of snobbery has turned out for the best, for the Royal Burgh of Inveraray is considered one of the most picturesque examples of 18th-century building in Scotland.

Fortunately, Inveraray Town Council decided to preserve the appearance of the capital of Argyll when there was a danger of modern building on old sites. So, instead of knocking down the fine old houses, they had them reconstructed, so that the insides were modernised, while the outsides remained the same (only cleaner) as they had been for 200 years. Besides the old buildings, the church and the fancy bridge across the River Shira are also 18th century.

At the head of the quay is a Celtic Cross, and you can walk up to the great archway by the Argyll Arms Hotel to a fine beech avenue which takes you to Essachosen Glen. If you are there at the right time you will hear one of the prides of Inveraray, the peal of bells installed at the beginning of this century by Niall Diarmid, the tenth Duke of Argyll.

Inveraray Castle was started in 1746, but was not completed until 1877. After a fire in the castle, the Duke of Argyll decided to add a top storey and the conical caps you see today. Before these were added, though, Sir Walter Scott (who built his own Abbotsford and was therefore something of an authority) described the castle as 'a massive and uniform edifice'.

Nowadays Inveraray Castle is open to the public on most days from May to September and, if you are lucky, you may see MacCailean Mor himself. That is the Gaelic title of the Duke of Argyll. It means 'Son of Great Colin', and goes back to the Campbell who founded the family fortune in the 13th century, Sir Colin.

The outstanding feature of the castle is the great hall, with its amazing display of weapons, targes and suits of armour. There are also historical relics, Beauvais tapestries, family portraits and some particularly fine mantelpieces and door frames by the Adam brothers.

The hill behind the castle is Duniquoich and the outlook tower on its top was known to the Commandos and Navymen who trained and were quartered at Inveraray as 'the airmen's canteen'!

North of Inveraray is a monument to its most famous son, Neil Munro, the novelist. He often used Inveraray as a background for his historical novels, and not far up Loch Fyne is Dunderave Castle, which he rechristened 'Doom Castle'. It was restored and is still occupied.

From Inveraray you can go south along the shore of Loch Fyne and down to the Mull of Kintyre. There is still a Loch Fyne fishing fleet, and you can still see little puffers making for Ardrishaig to go through the Crinan Canal, just as in the days of Neil Munro's immortal *Para Handy* stories. In Loch Fyne itself the Ministry of Agriculture and Fisheries carry out experiments, particularly on the movements of the herring.

7. Oban

Oban is often described as the 'Charing Cross of the Highlands', and it is true that you can get from Oban by land or sea to almost everywhere in the Highlands and to most of the Western Isles. But Oban is set in the midst of most surpassing beauty, which is more, I venture to suggest, than can be said of the original Charing Cross.

It is very much a town for the tourists, with many hotels and shops. Two hills look over it. On the top of one is a kind of Colosseum, which some unkind people call 'McCaig's Folly', under the impression that it has never been finished. Actually, McCaig was a rich man who had this tower built in the 1890's to provide work for the unemployed of the town. The other eminence is Pulpit Hill and from it you get wonderful views of the islands dotted over the sea.

Along the promenade you can visit the new Roman Catholic Cathedral, designed by Sir Giles Scott, and see the ancient Dunollie Castle, the home of the MacDougalls who were such enemies of Robert the Bruce.

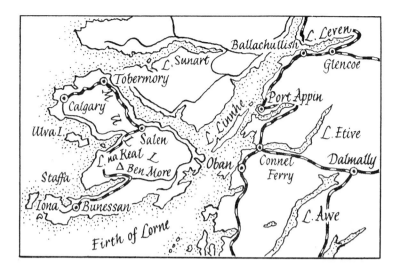

About four miles north is Dunstaffnage Castle and this is supposed to be the site of the capital of Dalriada. The Stone of Destiny was kept here until 850, when it was removed to Scone. For 500 years the Kings of Scotland were crowned upon it. Then Edward I of England, 'the Hammer of the Scots', took it to London, where it was made the seat of the Coronation Throne.

Easily the most popular sail from Oban is the cruise round the Isle of Mull, which includes visits to Staffa and Iona. Sometimes it is not possible to land on Staffa, or even on little, flat Iona (which is dealt with in my next piece). Staffa can be reached only by small boat from the steamer. You land at your own risk and, though there is a path into Fingal's Cave and a protecting rope, the Atlantic surging in can be quite frightening.

Staffa is a mighty mass of black basalt, and its black columns rise from the Atlantic like the pipes of a gigantic organ. There are several caves on the island, but the famous one is Fingal's Cave, which is sixty feet high and 220 feet deep. Probably the most famous visitor to Staffa was the composer, Felix Bartholdy Mendelssohn, who was so impressed that he wrote that oft-played overture, *Fingal's Cave*.

I wonder if Mendelssohn knew that the Gaelic name of Staffa was An Uamh Bhinn? The translation is 'the musical cave'. The old Highlanders heard the Atlantic echoing in the depths of Staffa and so chose a name that turned out to be prophetic.

8. Tobermory Bay

Tobermory, the capital of the Isle of Mull, is best known for the Tobermory Treasure, the Spanish galleon *Florida*, which lies in the bay and is supposed to contain most of the pay for the Spanish Armada. The Duke of Argyll, hereditary Lord High Admiral of Scotland, lays claim to the treasure and has already tried twice to reclaim it.

So far, all that has been brought up from the ship are some skulls, coins and a rusted cannon or two. There's no doubt that the ship is there. But some wise men are now saying that either it is not the *Florida*, or the *Florida* was not the pay ship.

But, if it brings you to the Isle of Mull, the Tobermory Treasure tale is worth it, for this is one of the wildest and most beautiful islands off the coast of Scotland. It is roughly thirty miles long and thirty miles broad. Tobermory is the only place of any size, but there are also the villages of Salen and Bunessan. Salen is below Ben More (3,185 feet), the highest peak on Mull.

From Tobermory—a famed yachting harbour, by the way—you can cross the island to Calgary. From Calgary many years ago Scots went out to settle in Canada and named the new settlement Calgary too.

Over on the west side Loch Tuath and Loch na Keal are separated by the Ulva's Isle named in Thomas Campbell's poem, *Lord Ullin's Daughter*. His Loch Goil is really Loch na Keal.

In the south there is the ancient Duart Castle, home of the Chief Scout, Sir Charles Maclean. Across Mull from Duart Castle is Fionnphort, where a passenger ferry runs to the fabled Iona, also reached by the cruise steamer from Oban. And here, I regret to say, I have to dispel an illusion.

Iona is repeatedly described as 'the cradle of Christianity in Scotland', because St Columba landed here in 563 and founded his church. But St Ninian landed at Whithorn in Galloway in 397 and founded the first Christian church in Scotland. There were quite a few saints in Scotland before St Columba came on the scene.

Nevertheless, Iona is worth visiting. It is a tiny island, but you can walk up the Street of the Dead to Reilig Oran where some sixty kings of Scotland, Ireland and Norway lie buried. The last Scottish king buried there was none other than Macbeth. The one before him was, naturally, King Duncan. St Margaret of Scotland is also buried there. She built St Oran's Chapel, which is just beside Iona Cathedral.

Iona Cathedral, built in the 12th century, has been restored by the devoted efforts of the Iona Community, led by Sir George MacLeod, who prefers to be known as the Reverend George MacLeod.

If you have time, climb Dun-I, Iona's highest peak. It is all of 332 feet high.

Loch Leven and the Glencoe Hills

Across Loch Leven lie the hills of Glencoe, standing sentinel round the 'Glen of Weeping'. This is surely the most famous, or infamous, of all Scottish glens, for every visitor to Scotland has heard something of the Massacre of Glencoe. There have been worse massacres in Scotland and more have been killed, but it is the infamy of the guests who turned upon their hosts that causes a thrill of horror among those who pass through Glencoe today. Charles Dickens admitted that he was terrified, but he had the advantage of stormy weather.

To the right of our picture you see the Isle of St Munda and on it is the burial place of the MacDonalds, who were massacred by the Campbells. Among those who lie there is John MacDonald, son of the MacIan, the chief who was shot as he called for wine for his visitors. The attackers pulled the rings off his wife's hands with their teeth, then stripped her and turned her out in a blizzard of snow. She died next day.

Yet Campbell of Glenlyon and his soldiers had been the guests of the MacDonalds in Glencoe for two weeks. Campbell bore secret orders to finish off the MacDonalds because, it was said, MacIan was too late in swearing his oath of allegiance to King William. All the clan chiefs had to take this oath by December 31st, 1691. Those who were loyal to the exiled King James delayed taking the oath until they got permission from the Stewart monarch.

MacDonald of Glencoe did not get this word until December 29th. Then he set out in terrible weather for Fort William. He arrived there on December 31st, but the governor of the fort told him he could not receive the oath because he was not a civil magistrate. He sent MacIan to Inveraray, with a letter to Sir Colin Campbell, Sheriff of Argyll, explaining the situation.

On January 6th, 1692, MacIan took the oath of allegiance, and Sir Colin Campbell sent the certificate to Edinburgh. In his turn, he explained that MacIan had turned up at Fort William on December 31st, ready to take the oath.

The Earl of Stair and some other Privy Councillors decided that an example should be made of the Mac-Donalds, and the secret orders for the massacre were sent out. One story is that the original order was written on a playing card, the nine of diamonds. To this day the nine of diamonds is known as 'The Curse of Scotland'.

Campbell of Glenlyon and his men arrived in Glencoe on February 1st. He explained to MacIan that he came in peace and he was all the more believed because he was related to the chief—his niece was married to Alexander MacDonald, the younger son of MacIan. Campbell's men were housed and entertained by the MacDonalds. Then at five o'clock in the morning of February 13th they attacked, shooting their hosts and setting fire to their houses.

Some of the MacDonalds escaped into the hills and died in the blizzard. A few escaped altogether. But, when the troops had gone and the MacDonalds came back, they found burning ruins and no cattle. Some 900 black cattle had been driven off, on Government orders.

There has been bad blood between the MacDonalds and the Campbells ever since. When I was at school in Glasgow, our teacher had to put James MacDonald on one side of the classroom and Alexander Campbell on the other, or they would have fought there and then. They often fought in the playground.

A modern Scottish historian, however, says that the Campbells were merely acting under orders and that the real villain was not even the Earl of Stair. He says it was King William himself. But try telling that to a MacDonald!

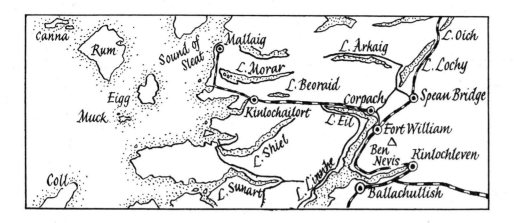

10. Ballachulish

Ballachulish is considered by many a visitor to Scotland as one of the funny names, along with Auchtermuchty and Ecclefechan and Milngavie (which, I had better explain, is pronounced 'Milguy'!). But Ballachulish is an exact description of the place. In the Gaelic it is *Bhaile aig a Chaolas*, which means 'township on the narrows'.

The village of Ballachulish stands on the south shore of Loch Leven, and the Ballachulish Ferry is placed at a strategic point which will save you some nineteen miles motoring round the loch. Mind you, motoring round the loch is no hardship. The scenery is wonderful and the road is good. But people in a hurry take their cars across on the Ballachulish Ferry.

Near the ferry slip is a rock and at the top of that rock you will find a partly hidden monument to James Stewart of the Glens, who was hanged for the murder of Colin Campbell of Glenure ('The Red Fox') in the wood of Lettermore in 1752. This is the spot where he was hanged, and for years his bones hung from the gibbet, always under a strong guard.

James of the Glens was tried by a Campbell judge and a Campbell jury in the Campbell stronghold of Inveraray, and most people then and even today consider him innocent of the Appin Murder. The name of the real murderer is known in Appin, but kept secret. Every now and then the Appin Murder comes up in the Scottish newspapers, theories are put forward, and names are bandied about. Robert Louis Stevenson used a version of the story in *Kidnapped*.

You will be glad to know that the Stewarts eventually got hold of the bones of James of the Glens, and they are buried in the ruined church of Keil, near Lettermore wood where 'The Red Fox' was shot.

The village of Ballachulish itself is an odd place because of the piles of slates which surround it. Ballachulish slates were once as famous as Bonawe granite, but the slate business has declined.

If Ballachulish looks rather odd amid the magnificent scenery, the town of Kinlochleven, at the top of the loch, looks even odder. It is an industrial centre, set in the midst of mountains. An aluminium factory provides the main work for the area: Kinlochleven is not beautiful, and yet the workers here have trout and salmon fishing, mountaineering, hiking and boating on their doorstep.

Loch Leven is part of the boundary between Argyllshire and Inverness-shire. It is a fiord which strikes inland from Loch Linnhe. This Loch Leven should not be confused with the Loch Leven in Kinross-shire, which is famous for fishing competitions and the fact that Mary Queen of Scots was imprisoned there in 1567, nor with the two River Levens in the south, nor the town of Leven on the Firth of Forth. I think it wise to warn you about this, because there is often great confusion among the Levens.

There are mighty mountains all round Loch Leven. The two peaks of Ben Vair, which tower over Ballachulish, are over 3,000 feet. At Kinlochleven the mountains are so high and so close that in midwinter the sun never shines on the town.

1. Ben Nevis from Corpach

We are looking across from the village of Corpach on Loch Eil. This loch joins Loch Linnhe and, at the foot of Ben Nevis in the distance, you can see Fort William, the main town in this part of the world. At the time of the troubles in the Highlands, General Monk built a fort here and named it after King William III.

Fort William is a holiday place and it also has a distillery, a West Highland Museum, and an aluminium works. Long pipes stretch down the side of Ben Nevis to bring water to these works.

Here we are at the start of the Great Glen, which runs right across Scotland to Inverness and the Moray Firth. It's the start also of the Great Glen Cattle Ranch, where you may see Scottish cowboys round up the herd. And it's the start of the Caledonian Canal, which follows the line of the Great Glen and links up Loch Lochy, Loch Oich and the far-famed Loch Ness. Over on the left of our picture you can see the start of Neptune's Staircase, the system of lochs by which vessels rise from the level of Loch Eil to the level of the canal.

James Watt, the inventor of the steam engine, surveyed this area for a canal as far back at 1773. But Thomas Telford did not start building until 1803. It was opened for shipping in 1848, but it was too shallow and had to be deepened. It was successfully opened in the following year and became a vital link between the east and the west. In those days vessels were often not seaworthy enough to attempt the rounding of Cape Wrath.

Today, though, most shipping can take Cape Wrath in their stride, so to speak, and only small boats go by the Caledonian Canal. Even so, the twenty-nine locks are proving too small for the job.

Neptune's Staircase rises eighty feet from Loch Eil to the Caledonian Canal. It's worth your while having a look at the intricate series of locks invented by Telford to overcome this problem.

The paradox of Ben Nevis is that, although it is the highest mountain in the whole of Britain, it doesn't seem nearly as tall as some of the lesser Munros. A Munro is the title the climbing fraternity give to mountains of over 3,000 feet, and comes from the name of the man who set out to climb and catalogue them. Ben Nevis is 4,406 feet from sea level, and it's from sea level we look at it here. Its base is about twenty-four miles round.

There is a fairly easy track leading right to the summit, where once an observatory and a hotel stood. There are also some very difficult ascents, and the Ben regularly takes its toll of inexperienced climbers. It's customary to allow four hours for the climb up, and three for the descent. At the annual Ben Nevis race the cross-country runners do the whole job in under two hours.

The reason Ben Nevis doesn't seem to rise to its full height is that it is composed of a rounded massif with no peaks. We always associate height with peaks. But anyone who climbs Ben Nevis will be quite sure that it's the highest mountain in Britain because the weather so often changes by the time you get to the top. This is one of the principal reasons for the incidence of accidents on the Ben.

12. Loch Lochy

It's historically right that we should see Loch Lochy with the winter snow around it, for near here was fought one of the great victories of the Marquis of Montrose, the Battle of Inverlochy. Loch Lochy, the first loch in the chain of the Caledonian Canal, is ten miles long and is linked with Loch Oich on the west.

There is a canal link with Loch Eil on the east, but the natural outflow of Loch Lochy is by the River Lochy to Loch Linnhe. Inverlochy, represented now by a castle, stands on the banks of the River Lochy.

Montrose and his Royalist Highlanders were fighting the Covenanters where and when they found them. Early in 1645 he'd raided the Campbell country round Loch Awe with great effect. The Campbell chief, the Duke of Argyll, was all the more determined to defeat Montrose. There had been enmity between them since they were students at St Andrew's University.

Argyll worked it out that Montrose was bound to go into the Great Glen, so he arranged with General Baillie of the Covenanters' army at Inverness that the General would bring his forces down the Glen, while Argyll would bring his men up from the south and so seal Montrose off.

Montrose, moving up the Great Glen, learned that Baillie was in front of him and Argyll behind him. What was he to do? In the words of John Buchan he accomplished 'one of the great exploits in the history of British arms'. Despite the snow and the blizzards he marched his Highlanders over the mountains from Loch Ness until they reached the slopes of Ben Nevis, overlooking Argyll and his Campbells below.

It was February 1st, 1645, and Montrose and his men camped in the snow without any fires. They could see the Campbell fires and they could also see a galley on Loch Lochy. This was where Argyll slept. He wouldn't take the chance of sleeping where Montrose's men could catch him, and he left a junior member of the Campbell family in charge.

In the morning, Candlemas Day, Montrose ordered his trumpet to sound. This was a blast the Campbells knew well, and dreaded. But, before they could ready themselves for battle, the Highlanders streamed down the snow-clad mountainside upon them. The Campbells might have rallied, but they saw their leader, Argyll himself, sailing away up Loch Lochy in his galley and they had not the heart to fight for a runaway commander.

It is said that the Campbell dead numbered 1,500, while Montrose lost only four men. It was also said for many years that no one could emulate the marches and the deeds of Montrose and his men. But, during World War Two, the Commandos trained here, and they did everything that Montrose did, though they were preparing for battle instead of actually fighting an enemy. Perhaps the Commandos did even more than Montrose, for never were men so trained.

They are remembered today in the Commando Memorial on the way to Loch Lochy and about a mile from Spean Bridge. This is one of the most effective monuments in Scotland and thousands of people visit it every year. It was designed by Scott Sutherland, and was formally unveiled by Queen Elizabeth, the Queen Mother, in 1951.

13. Loch Beoraid

The Road from Fort William to Mallaig goes by a line of lochs, and Loch Beoraid is the least known of them. That's because it is hidden from the road. So is Loch Morar, the last of the lochs, although it is only three-quarters of a mile from the road. But you know of Loch Morar because the little River Morar rushes from it, under the road bridge, into the Sound of Sleat.

Beoraid is a beautiful little loch, with good fishing, and you might be a hundred miles away from civilisation when you are on its shores. It is one of the four inland lochs on this route, for most are connected with the sea, directly or by river.

First, as you go up from Fort William towards Mallaig, you travel by the side of Loch Eil, an off-shoot of Loch Linnhe. Then you come to long and lonely Loch Shiel, and from the road you see the monument set up in memory of Prince Charles Edward Stewart. Bonnie Prince Charlie stands on top of a stone column, placed at the very spot where he set up his standard on August 19th, 1745. This is Glenfinnan, and it was here the great adventure started that was to restore the Stewarts to the throne, the adventure which ended in defeat at Culloden on April 16th, 1746. There is an inscription on the monument in Gaelic, Latin and English.

You go by Kinlochailort, at the head of Loch Ailort, to the breath-taking beauty of Arisaig, where the sun shines on silver sands and seas of Mediterranean blue.

The road turns north to Morar, and Loch Morar is just behind it. Loch Morar is certainly the deepest piece of water in Britain, and it is deeper than any piece of water in Europe, with the single exception of a submarine valley off the south of Scandinavia. The depth of Loch Morar is 180 fathoms, well over 1,000 feet. The loch is about twelve miles long, and it is a mere thirty feet above sea level.

At the west end of Loch Morar there is a group of four small islands. After the Battle of Culloden, Lord Lovat escaped, but he was captured two months later on one of these islands.

Loch Morar has a monster in it, and it has been seen several times, though not nearly as often as the Loch Ness Monster. Descriptions of the Morar monster are reasonably like the average description of the Loch Ness Monster, and Tim Dinsdale, in his book about Loch Ness, thinks both monsters are of the same family of prehistoric creatures. He considers that conditions in both lochs are much the same and that the great depth helps the monster family to survive.

North of Mallaig, up the Sound of Sleat, is Loch Hourn (Gaelic for 'Loch of Hell'), where a monster has also been reported on various occasions. Tim Dinsdale records this monster in his book too, but it is unlikely to be of the Loch Ness Monster family because Hourn, unlike Ness and Morar, is a sea loch.

If you see the Loch Morar monster, be sure to give the newspapers a ring. And if you photograph it, you can name your own price!

We go to Mallaig, a fishing port with a passenger service to Skye and the Western Isles. Mallaig could hardly be called beautiful, but from it you can see some of the finest views in Scotland.

14. Eigg and Rhum

This is an unusual view of what the guide-book writers persist in calling the 'cocktail islands'—Rhum and Eigg, pronounced 'rum' and 'egg'. It is taken from Ardtae, Acharacle, on Loch Shiel, and it shows Eigg directly in front of Rhum. But the passenger on the steamer sailing from Mallaig sees the comparatively low-lying Eigg to his left and the peaks of Rhum directly in front of him.

Eigg is the most populated of the three islands at which the steamer calls—Eigg, Rhum and Canna, in that order. The population is in the region of eighty. Although Eigg looks fairly flat from a distant view, it has high, basaltic cliffs and a strange looking mountain at one end of the island. This is Sgurr of Eigg (1,289 feet) and at its top are 400 feet high columns of black glassy basalt, which a volcano threw up thousands of years ago.

The jetty at Eigg is unsuitable for steamers, so passengers, luggage and mail are taken off in a small motor boat.

In the 16th century all the inhabitants of Eigg were MacDonalds, and they had some sort of feud with the MacLeods of Skye. The MacLeods sailed for Eigg to teach the MacDonalds a lesson, but word came to the island that the Skye warriors were on their way, led by none other than the Lord of the Isles himself. The MacDonalds, outnumbered, decided not to fight and they gathered—men, women, children, cattle and household pets—in a great cave on the south-east coast.

At first the MacLeods could not find them and had to be content with burning the MacDonalds' houses. Then, as they searched the island, they heard either a baby cry or a dog bark in the cave (historians diverge on this point). So the MacLeods brought brushwood along and lit fires in the mouth of the cave. The smoke blew into the cave and the whole population of Eigg was suffocated.

Across the Sound of Eigg, to the south, is the island of Muck. It is almost impossible to land on Muck and there is no population there.

The steamer goes by the Sound of Rhum, with the Isle of Skye to the north, to a sheltered bay in the middle of the Rhum coast. Once again the jetty can't take a steamer and a motor boat comes out. Rhum is a nature reserve and, although it's the largest island in the group (eight miles long by seven miles wide), it has a population of about forty. In 1826 the entire population, with the exception of one family, were forced to emigrate. As on Eigg and Canna, there is no such thing as a hotel.

Askival (2,659 feet) is the highest of the peaks of Rhum, and there are three other mountains of over 2,000 feet.

Round the cliff coast of Rhum you sail to Canna, the only island of this group which has a proper pier. Canna is the smallest of these isles, and some think the prettiest (though that's maybe not just the best word to describe the scenery around here). It's four and a half miles long, but only three-quarters of a mile broad.

Canna is famous for Compass Hill (690 feet), basalt cliffs at the east of the island. The deposits of iron in Compass Hill are so rich that they affect the compasses of passing ships.

The population is around twenty-five, but this is frequently increased by fishing crews from various parts of Europe. It has become traditional for each crew to paint the name of their ship in bright letters on the cliff face behind the pier. Some of the names are in such seemingly inaccessible places that it's apparent that the modern fisherman is also a circus acrobat.

5. The Coolins

Speed, bonnie boat, like a bird on the wing.
  Onward, the sailors cry.
Carry the lad who's born to be king
  Over the sea to Skye.

But the Highlanders who were supposed to sing that song were too optimistic. True, baffled their foes stood by the shore, follow they did not dare. But Bonnie Prince Charlie was not 'born to be king' after all, and his journey over the sea to Skye saved his life, but nothing more.

Thousands and thousands of people have travelled over the sea to Skye since then and they all talk with awe of that great mountain range, the Coolins. This view of the Coolins shows those legendary hills in contrast with the pastoral and peaceful side of the Isle of Skye. In the centre is the peak of Blaven (3,042 feet).

Blaven is a mysterious mountain. It's known to climbers as a 'killer' hill. It has inspired more poems than any other Scottish peak. And it's said to have a magnetic power so strong that it knocks compasses silly. On the subject of climbing, by the way, the Coolins are regarded as the finest climbs in Britain. But you should not climb there unless you are an experienced mountaineer or are with one.

I use the spelling Coolins because that is the style adopted by their owner, Dame Flora Macleod of Macleod. But the experts say that the proper spelling is Cuchullins.

The legend is that a goddess named Skiach was the first being to inhabit these mountains. She gave her name to the island, and Skiach was shortened to Skye. Skiach started a battle school for heroes in the mountains, and it became so famous that the greatest warrior in the world heard about it. He was an Irishman, of course. His name was Cuchullin, the Hero of Ulster.

Cuchullin decided to visit this woman who had never been conquered in battle. He took three strides from the north of Ireland and landed at the battle school. Nobody there had ever heard of him, so he proceeded to take on Skiach's hero students one by one and beat them all. Skiach now deigned to notice him, and she allowed him, as a special treat, to fight her daughter. Cuchullin fought Skiach's daughter for two days and then she gave in.

This annoyed Skiach, who came down from her mountain top and set out to teach Cuchullin a lesson. They fought all over Skye for two days, but it was a draw. Then Skiach summoned all the heroes to watch the second round, for she said they would never see a fight like this again. So Cuchullin and Skiach once again joined battle, and they fought for two days but it was still a draw.

By this time Skiach's daughter was getting worried about the possible outcome of the fight, so she made a cheese and asked the contestants to taste it. But they kept on fighting. Then she roasted a deer, but still they fought. So she gathered the hazel-nuts of knowledge, roasted them and stuffed a second roasted deer with them. This time Skiach and Cuchullin accepted her invitation to dine, because each had a secret thought that the hazel-nuts would give him or her the knowledge of how to outwit the other.

But, when they ate, the wisdom came to them that neither would ever beat the other, so they made peace. Cuchullin went back to Ireland, and Skiach called their fighting ground 'Cuchullin's Hills'.

16. Macleod's Tables

Across Dunvegan Loch in the Isle of Skye we see the twin hills which are called Macleod's Tables. The legend is that they were not always flat topped. When St Columba came from Iona to convert Skye to Christianity, he visited a chief who lived in a fort on Loch Bracadale. According to the rules of Highland hospitality, he should have been offered bed and board. But the chief feared the introduction of Christianity and so, when St Columba had finished his sermon, he ordered him and his followers out of the castle.

As the saint was thrust out of the gate, the earth rocked and a great cloud of dust arose. When it cleared, the chief and his men saw that the two peaks behind the fort had become flat-topped hills—a bed and a table for St Columba.

How did St Columba's Table get the name of Macleod's Table, then? Well, the story here is that one of the Macleod chiefs was on a visit to the King—some say in London, but it is much more likely to have been the King of Scotland in Edinburgh. When he was royally entertained to dinner and saw the magnificence of his surroundings, he was duly impressed. But the King was unwise enough to say to him, 'Have you ever seen a larger table? Have you ever seen bigger candlesticks?'

This was too much for a Skye man. The Macleod replied that, if the King would be good enough to visit him at Dunvegan Castle, he would show His Majesty an even larger table and even bigger candlesticks. The King took him at his word, and visited the Macleod at Dunvegan the following year. The castle is compact rather than big, and the King could not see where it could house a larger table and bigger candlesticks than he had.

But that evening the Macleod led the way to Healaval Beg (the Gaelic name of the nearer hill in our picture), and there on the perfectly flat top the dinner was spread out—a far greater dinner table than the King could imagine. Behind each guest stood a tall clansman of the Clan Macleod, holding up a lighted torch—and each was two or three times the height of the King's candlesticks.

After that the name of Macleod's Tables was given to both hills. And the moral of the story is—never try to put one over on a Skye man!

There are dozens of fairy stories and legends about this part of the Isle of Skye. Once you cross the Fairy Bridge on your way to Dunvegan, anything can happen.

In Dunvegan Castle (open to the public at certain times) you can see the Fairy Flag of the Macleods. It was given to the Macleods by the fairies and, if they were ever in danger, they had only to wave the flag and they would win the day. But they were limited to three waves. The flag has been waved twice and on each occasion the spell worked. So the Macleods still have a wave up their sleeve.

The Macleods have lived in Dunvegan Castle for more than 700 years. Dame Flora Macleod of Macleod is the octogenarian chief of the clan, and her successor is her grandson, John Macleod of Macleod. Each successor to the chieftainship is supposed to drain Rory Mor's horn at a draught. Rory Mor was Sir Roderick Macleod, twelfth chief of the clan, and his horn holds nearly half a gallon. On his twenty-first birthday, John Macleod of Macleod accomplished the feat. He drank nearly half a gallon of claret at one draught.

Dunvegan Castle has walls nine to ten feet thick. It has also the only dungeon I know where you take a step *up* to reach it. The last time it was used was in the 18th century, when a Macleod chief put his wife into it so that he could marry another woman.

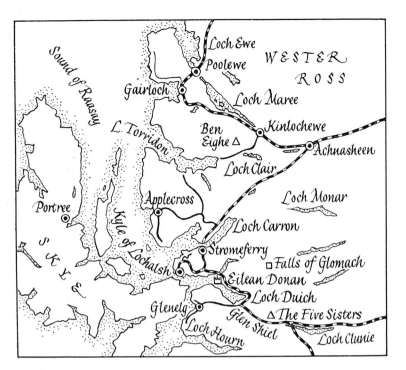

17. Loch Duich

The Scots, who argue about everything, naturally argue about scenery. Lowlanders say that the most beautiful loch in Scotland is Loch Lomond. Highlanders swear by Loch Maree. But many visitors to Scotland think that Loch Duich in Wester Ross is the most bewitching piece of water they have seen anywhere.

This picture is taken from the clachan of Letterfearn (a name derived from the Gaelic and meaning 'the alder side'), looking across Loch Duich at that magnificent group of mountains, the Five Sisters of Kintail. The tallest of the girls is 3,505 feet. Much of the ground round here belongs to the Scottish National Trust, so will be preserved for all time.

Loch Duich was once known as Loch Duthick, and it's believed that it was named after a St Duthec. Although it's a sea loch, there's less salt water in it than the average Scottish fiord. The Atlantic comes in by Kyle of Lochalsh, the gateway to Skye, and Loch Duich starts at Dornie, where you can visit the restored castle of Eilean Donan. The castle stands on a small island and you reach it by a fine old stone bridge.

Eilean Donan was built in the 13th century and Alexander III of Scotland presented it to Colin Fitzgerald for distinguished service 'by sea and land' after the Battle of Largs

in 1263. In this battle the Scots overthrew the Vikings, who retired hurt and gave up their claims to Scottish land. The castle became a stronghold of the Mackenzie Clan, but it was shattered by English cannon after the Battle of Glenshiel in 1719.

If you are coming from the south, you go through Glenshiel to reach Loch Duich. The battle was a strange one. It was fought by the wild Macraes, a local clan, assisted by Rob Roy and some of his men, and 400 Spaniards, on the Jacobite side, versus the British Government's troops. When the Government troops attacked, the Spaniards laid down their arms without firing a single shot. Rob Roy wasn't of much help either. The Royalists tossed hand grenades into the heather and set it on fire, and the Macraes were eventually defeated.

Glenshiel comes from the Gaelic too and, according to the expert, it can mean 'Glen of the cattle', 'Glen of the hunting', or 'Glen of the rain'. I trust it doesn't mean the last when you are there.

Like other parts of the Highlands, this district was famous for its illicit stills. Yet it was recorded in the *Scottish Statistical Account*, published in 1845, that 'in a population of 1,200 souls, there is only one drunkard'.

The people of Loch Duich and Kintail were regarded as the tallest in all the Highlands. Many of them emigrated to America in the 19th century, and the average height is just average now.

If you have the opportunity, you can visit in the vicinity the Falls of Glomach, the highest in Britain. The estimated height is 350 feet, which makes Glomach more than twice the height of Niagara.

It is said that, in south-westerly gales, the water of Loch Duich is sometimes blown so high in the air that the loch looks like a boiling cauldron. I cannot claim to have seen this myself, but you may be lucky.

18. Loch Clair

The tiny clachan of Achnasheen—a railway station, a hotel, and a house or two—is the entrance to a magical part of Scotland, Wester Ross. A climbing expert has described Wester Ross as having the wildest scenery and the grandest mountains on the mainland of Scotland, and I wouldn't dare to disagree.

From Achnasheen you go north-west to Kinlochewe and a cross-roads. Straight ahead is beautiful Loch Maree, the subject of our next picture. But if you take the road to the left, the one to Torridon, you enter a wonderful region of little lochs and giant peaks.

Just off the road between Kinlochewe and Torridon there is this little jewel of a lake, Loch Clair. It is connected by a channel to another miniature loch, Loch Coulin. From these exquisite pieces of water you get some of the best views of the mighty Ben Eighe, which is made up of seven or eight peaks. The highest peak is 3,369 feet, but mountains in Scotland often appear higher than they really are because you are nearly always seeing them from about sea level.

No matter what time of the year you see Ben Eighe, it appears to have snow on it. True, it very often has snow on its peaks, but in the height of the summer the snow effect comes from the fact that the upper part of Ben Eighe is formed of white quartzite. The broken screes glisten in the summer sun and look just like snow.

The mountains hereabouts are often compared to the Alps, though they are not nearly as high. They are just as difficult, however, and only practised climbers should tackle them.

Much of the country round here is a Nature Reserve. There is fine salmon and trout fishing in all the lochs and, though Loch Maree is the best known, little lochs like Clair and Coulin can give wonderful sport too.

If you go on from Loch Clair, you come to the village of Torridon and you can go no farther, unless you take the track which leads to the two Youth Hostels on Loch Torridon.

You are far out of the world here and, although the houses you see are comparatively modern and certainly comfortable, it's not difficult to imagine the days, just over 100 years ago, when the houses were built of stone with turf roofs.

Each house was divided into a byre on one side and a living room on the other. The family and their cattle were under the same roof and they entered by the same door. The family ate potatoes and herring twice a day and had porridge for supper.

Today the people of Wester Ross have better houses and eat in a much better (though still simple) style. But there are not nearly as many people living in this airt as there were in primitive days.

19. Loch Maree

One of the most enchanting sights in Scotland, a country notable for enchanting sights, is the view of Loch Maree which you see when you motor from Kinlochewe to Gairloch. This is by far the best way to see Loch Maree. The journey in the opposite direction has its charms, but it means you must constantly be turning round to get the best view. And this is not recommended on roads in Wester Ross.

Loch Maree, famous for its fishing, is eighteen miles long and, on an average, one and a half miles broad. It is guarded on the north by the huge bulk of Slioch (or Sliabhach), a mountain 3,217 feet high. The loch has never been known to freeze, but this is not surprising, since it is sixty fathoms deep. Indeed, Loch Maree is one of the deepest pieces of water in Europe.

There are twenty-four wooded islands on Loch Maree. The most famous is Eilean Maree, about the centre of the loch. On it is an ancient burying ground and a deep well. Around it are all sorts of stories and theories.

It is said that the burying ground was dedicated to the Virgin Mary, hence the name of the loch and the island. But another story is that some Norse kings are buried here and the real name is Eilean nan Righ, the 'Island of the Kings'. Then there's the romantic story of the Norse prince and princess who married and then had to flee from parental wrath. They were caught and slain on the island, and two of the graves are supposed to be theirs.

Yet another story is that a monastery once stood on the island and it was founded by a St Maree from Iona. There seems to be no doubt that a godly man named Maree did live in this district, and he was called St Maree after he died. His is the well in the centre of the island. Up to the year 1845 it was the practice around Loch Maree to take an insane person to Eilean Maree and make him drink from the well. Then he was tied to a boat and rowed right round the island. This was supposed to be a 'cure'.

Another island, Eilean Suthainn, is worthy of mention. Although it is only a mile long, it has three lochans on it.

As we go on to Gairloch, we are in the region of the golden eagle. Gairloch itself is one of the few mainland districts where the grey lag goose nests, and that sturdy chap with the binoculars may well be Peter Scott!

Gairloch is a charming holiday place, with a harbour for fishing boats and beautiful sands. It was once a great smuggling district and a centre for illicit stills. In the Thirties of last century the parish minister commended a local laird for starting up a distillery and putting a legal business in place of the illicit one.

From Gairloch you go to Poolewe, where the River Ewe is the link between Loch Maree and Loch Ewe. Not far away are the Inverewe Gardens, visited by people from all over the world because of the wonderful collection of sub-tropical trees, shrubs and flowers. They are administered by the National Trust for Scotland.

On my last visit to Inverewe I met Germans, Americans, French, Japanese and Norwegians, all amazed that such flowers and trees could grow so beautifully in the north of Scotland.

20. Standing Stones of Callanish

Scotland has its own Stonehenge, the Standing Stones of Callanish (or Callernish) on the Isle of Lewis. From the capital of Lewis, Stornoway, you travel fifteen miles east to the head of East Loch Roag. Callanish is one of the finest examples of a prehistoric stone circle. There are forty-seven stones, and the central one is a monolith eighteen feet high. The stone circle is 400 feet long from north to south.

The heath and moorland you see around the Stone Circle are typical of Lewis, whose Gaelic name is Eilean an Fhraoich, the Isle of Heather. Lewis is only part of the island, however; the lower part is Harris, and the proper name is Lewis and Harris. Lewis itself is about 100,000 acres of heathery moors. There are hardly any trees, although there are traces on the moorland of an ancient forest.

According to the Lewis story, this great forest was burned down by a Viking invader as part of a 'scorched earth policy'. The Vikings are also blamed for pulling the whole of the Long Island (the name applied to Lewis, Harris, North Uist, Benbecula, South Uist, Eriskay and Barra which, they say, were once all one) out of its original position.

At the extreme north of the Butt of Lewis, and near the lighthouse built by Robert Louis Stevenson's father, is a natural opening in the rock called the Eye of the Butt. The story is that the Long Island lay far to the south, but one of those Vikings put a tow-rope from his galley through the Eye and started pulling. He really wanted to take the Long Island home with him, but the rope broke just where Lewis is now.

Lewis and Harris were once owned by the great soap magnate, Lord Leverhulme. He had industrial plans for the island, but he had not counted on the independence of the islanders, who had a horror of being 'patronised'. So the only mementoes of Lord Leverhulme are the village of Leverburgh (formerly Obbe) in Harris, and Stornoway Castle, which he presented to the town when he left the island. It is now a well-equipped technical college. The grounds are open to the public, and include an eighteen-hole golf course.

Stornoway is a surprising town to find amid the moorland and the fishing burns and lochs. It has a big harbour, an airport near by, a fishing industry, and big woollen mills. The famous hand-woven Harris tweed is made in Lewis as well as Harris, and the exporting centre is at Stornoway. Harris tweed has many imitators, so you should make sure the trade-mark is on the tweed before you buy it.

If you want to see Harris tweed made on its own ground, you go south from Stornoway by Loch Seaforth, where the Seaforth Highlanders were mustered. You are in North Harris until you reach the narrow isthmus between East Loch Tarbert and West Loch Tarbert. On this third of a mile is Tarbert, the capital of Harris. You come across the name Tarbert in many parts of Western Scotland. It means a portage, and it is always applied to a place where there is only a small strip of land between two pieces of water.

The road from Tarbert runs through South Harris to Leverburgh and Rodel (or Rodil). At Rodel you should visit the 15th-century church of St Clement. It was once a priory and has been restored.

Butt of Lewis

L. Roag

Stornoway

Callanish

LEWIS

HARRIS

L. Seaforth

Tarbert

Leverburgh

Rodel

Lochmaddy

N. UIST

BENBECULA

S. UIST

ERISKAY

BARRA

21. Lochinver

Just as there are constant arguments as to which is the most beautiful loch in Scotland, there are debates as to where you will find the most fantastic scenery. Most people would swear by Wester Ross, but that is probably because most people have never ventured north of Ullapool to the west coast of Sutherland. Indeed, north of Ullapool is still a *terra incognita* to the vast majority of tourists.

Round the little port of Lochinver, at the head of Loch Inver, are three of the most fantastically shaped mountains you will see anywhere. They are Suilven, the sugar-loaf peak on the right of our picture, Canisp and Stac Polly. They are among the world's oldest mountains, and their odd shapes are due to their particular geological formation. To be technical, these mountains are Torridonian sandstone on a base of Lewisian gneiss. (If you learn this statement by heart, you can bring it out casually at the right moment and impress your fellow travellers no end!)

Suilven is 2,399 feet and a famous climb, but it is almost perpendicular on the Caisteal Liath side. Canisp is 2,786 feet and Stac Polly 2,009 feet, but, though none of them is a 'Munro', they look higher than many a peak of 3,000 feet and over.

You reach Lochinver from Inchnadamph, ten miles inland to the east. Another famous mountain, Ben More Assynt (3,273 feet), is your signpost. Inchnadamph is at the head of Loch Assynt, renowned for its brown trout. The road to Lochinver runs by the shore of Loch Assynt and passes the ruined remains of Ardvreck Castle, where the gallant Montrose was imprisoned for a while after he had been captured.

South of Inchnadamph is Allt-nan-Uamh, where the remains of Ice Age animals have been found in prehistoric caves. But parts of the scenery about here are so strange that it wouldn't surprise you in the least to see an Ice Age animal pop its head round a piece of Torridonian sandstone. Incidentally, Torridonian sandstone is the oldest stone known in the world.

If you go north from Lochinver you see all sorts of weird rock formations along the coast line. You look out on the magnificent Minch, between the mainland and the Isle of Lewis.

In the hinterland of this strange and rocky shore is the noted Reay Deer Forest, so that sportsmen of all kinds will find the west of Sutherland a place dear to their heart.

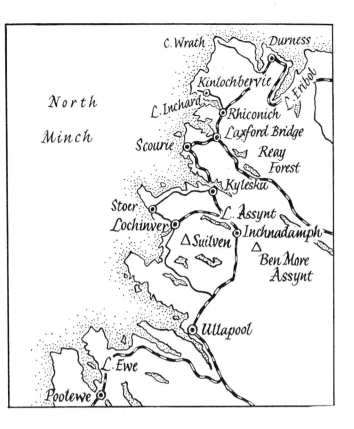

2. Durness

As you go up from Lochinver to Cape Wrath, the north-west point of Great Britain, you feel you are coming to the end of the world. And yet the name of the country is Sutherland, the South Land. It was given to this most northerly part of Britain by our old friends, the Vikings. As they sailed south from Scandinavia, this was the first mainland they encountered, and so they called it the Southern Land.

Seven miles north of Lochinver you come to Stoer, a crofting township on Stoer Bay. There is a lighthouse on Stoer Point, and from it you see the Old Man of Stoer, an oddly-shaped rock off the Point.

The road turns to the west, and you cross Loch Cairnbawn by the Kylesku car ferry. You are going north again now, and you arrive at another crofting township, Scourie. Out in the Minch to the north is one of the best-known wild bird sanctuaries in Scotland, the Island of Handa.

At Laxford Bridge there's a junction with the road from Lairg, and then it's straight for Durness and Cape Wrath. But at the clachan of Rhiconich it's worth while taking the little road to the left, which leads to a small fishing port called Kinlochbervie, on Loch Inchard. The fishing industry here is so important that an ice plant has been installed, to keep the fish fresh before it goes south to the cities.

Durness is the nearest place of any size to Cape Wrath, the end of our journey. It stands on a peninsula, with Loch Eriboll on one side of it and the Kyle of Durness on the other. It's a township of crofters, sheep farmers and fishers. By the way, if you are wondering just what a 'township' looks like, our picture of Durness gives a perfect example.

On a fine sandy bay a mile north-west of Durness is the 17th-century church, which contains many relics of the neighbourhood. In the kirkyard you will find a monument to the 'Robert Burns of the Highlands', the Gaelic poet, Rob Donn.

Near Durness is the Smoo Cave, a series of three limestone caverns which became famous when Sir Walter Scott wrote about them after a visit in 1814.

Behind Loch Eriboll to the south-west is the mountain of Cran Stackie, which is 2,630 feet, and yet is not as impressive as Cape Wrath itself, which is a mere 523 feet. But Cape Wrath is precipitous and the seas come roaring in towards this outpost of Britain.

The road to Cape Wrath and the lighthouse is not suitable for cars, unless they are the very tough type. You should either walk it or go by bicycle. But, however you get there, it's worth it when you do. This awe-inspiring point adds the final touch to the Glory of the West.